VIKINGS

Illustrated by
Brent Linley and Philip Hood

Edited by
Debbie Reid

Designed by
Claire Robertson

Picture research by
Helen Taylor

Consultant
Rose Croxford

CONTENTS

Vikings!

A thousand years ago, an Irish monk wrote a short verse in the margin of a book:

The wind is bitter tonight
It tosses the sea's white hair
I have no fear that fierce raiders
Will sail the seas on
such a night.

The 'fierce raiders' were Vikings, people who spread terror on the coasts of Europe each time they appeared in their dragon-headed warships.

The people whose lands they invaded often had no idea who they were or where they came from. They called them many different names: 'northmen', 'strangers', 'shipmen' and 'heathen men'. 'Vikings', meaning 'pirates', was just one of the names given to them.

FIRST VIKING LIGHTNING
RAIDS ON BRITISH ISLES
793

750

VIKINGS SETTLE IN
ORKNEYS AND SHETLAN

LAST VIKING
RAID ON ENGLAND
1151

1100
(11 hundred)

HARALD HARD RULER
OF NORWAY INVADES ENGLAI
AND IS KILLED IN BATTLE
1066

NORMANS CONQUER ENGLAI
1066

1200
(12 hundred)

1700
(17 hundred)

VIKING SAGAS
WRITTEN DOWN
1180s-1300

1500
(15 hundred)

1400
(14 hundred)

1300
(13 hundred)

1600
(16 hundred)

We still think of fierce raiders whenever we hear the word 'Vikings'. Even so, we now know a lot more about the other sides of Viking life. The Vikings were also explorers, traders, farmers and craftspeople. Nowadays, we know more about the peaceful life the Vikings lived in their homes.

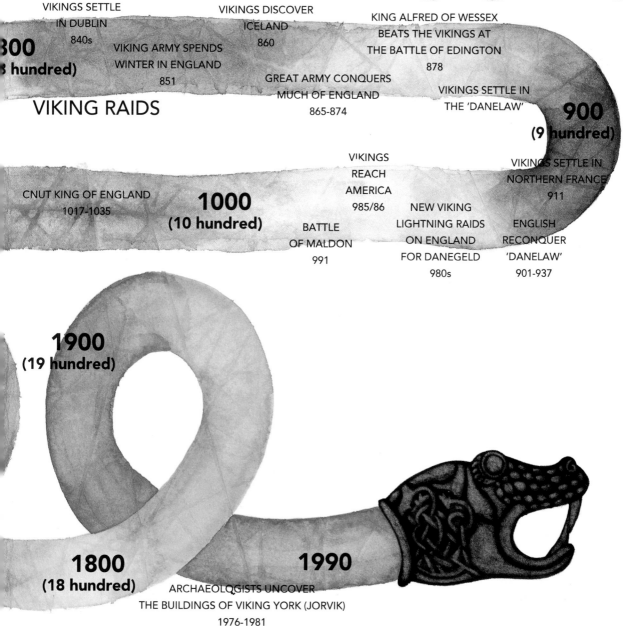

VIKINGS SETTLE
IN DUBLIN
840s

800
(8 hundred)

VIKING ARMY SPENDS
WINTER IN ENGLAND
851

VIKINGS DISCOVER
ICELAND
860

GREAT ARMY CONQUERS
MUCH OF ENGLAND
865-874

KING ALFRED OF WESSEX
BEATS THE VIKINGS AT
THE BATTLE OF EDINGTON
878

VIKINGS SETTLE IN
THE 'DANELAW'

VIKING RAIDS

900
(9 hundred)

CNUT KING OF ENGLAND
1017-1035

1000
(10 hundred)

BATTLE
OF MALDON
991

VIKINGS
REACH
AMERICA
985/86

NEW VIKING
LIGHTNING RAIDS
ON ENGLAND
FOR DANEGELD
980s

VIKINGS SETTLE IN
NORTHERN FRANCE
911

ENGLISH
RECONQUER
'DANELAW'
901-937

1900
(19 hundred)

1800
(18 hundred)

1990

ARCHAEOLOGISTS UNCOVER
THE BUILDINGS OF VIKING YORK (JORVIK)
1976-1981

The Viking world

The Vikings first came from Denmark, Norway and Sweden – the lands we call Scandinavia. After the year 790, many Vikings left these homelands and sailed east, west, south and north. Suddenly, it seemed as if the Vikings were everywhere.

Traders, raiders, settlers, explorers

Vikings from different lands sailed for different reasons.

Swedish Vikings were mainly interested in trade. They travelled east and south across the rivers of Russia, taking walrus tusks, furs and slaves down to the Black Sea. Here they traded them for silk, wine and jewellery.

The Vikings of Denmark and Norway were traders too, but they found it easier to get rich by raiding. They learned that lands to the west and south were wealthy and badly defended. They attacked the coasts of Europe, stealing treasure and capturing slaves. Later, they sailed back to the British Isles and Northern France, to conquer land and to settle down.

The Vikings of Norway were also explorers, looking for unknown lands. They sailed north-west and found lands which they named Iceland and Greenland. Norwegian Vikings then became the first Europeans to reach North America.

The world of the Vikings

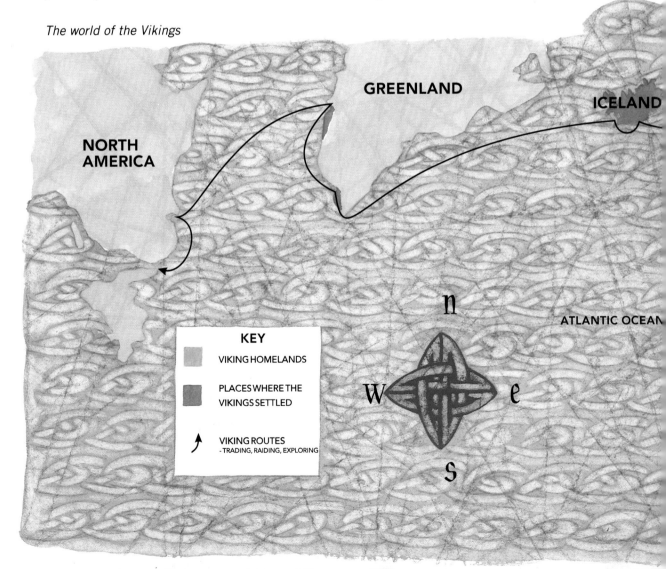

GREENLAND

ICELAND

NORTH AMERICA

ATLANTIC OCEAN

KEY

VIKING HOMELANDS

PLACES WHERE THE VIKINGS SETTLED

VIKING ROUTES – TRADING, RAIDING, EXPLORING

n

W e

s

Why did the Vikings appear?

People have suggested many reasons why the Vikings left home and suddenly appeared off the coasts of Europe in the 790s.

One important reason was that there was not much good farmland in their own countries. When a Viking farmer died, his eldest son took over the farm. Then the younger sons had to leave and look somewhere else to make a living. (Women only took over the farm if there were no sons.)

Many Vikings were forced to leave home, because of wars. In Norway in particular, different families were fighting for power. When a king was driven out, he would take his men with him and look for new lands to rule.

In earlier times, Viking ships were not very strongly built. It was only when they learned to build sea-going ships, in the 750s, that the Vikings were able to threaten other lands.

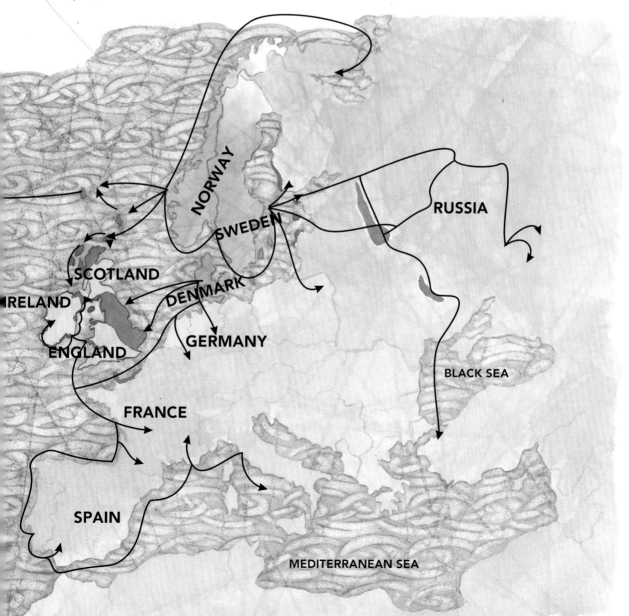

How do we know?

The Vikings who came to Britain did not write books about themselves. In order to find out what they did, and what they were like, we have to piece together evidence from many different places.

Monks wrote books about their enemies — the Vikings

Books by monks

When the Vikings came to England, the people who lived there were the Anglo-Saxons. Unlike the Vikings, the Anglo-Saxons did write books. Their books were written by monks – Christian holy men. This is what a monk called Simeon of Durham wrote about the Vikings:

And they came to the church of Lindisfarne, trampled the holy places, dug up the altars and seized all the treasures of the holy church. They killed some of the brothers; some they took away with them in chains; and some they drowned in the sea.

Monks like Simeon of Durham can tell us how the Vikings appeared to their enemies. They can't tell us, however, what the Vikings thought about themselves.

Sagas

Although the Vikings did not write books, they remembered the past through poems and stories. These were learned by heart and passed on from the old to the young. Eventually, many of the stories were written down in books called **sagas**. Saga writers were more interested in telling a good story than in writing accurate history.

This is a page from the saga about King Olaf of Norway

Digging for Vikings

Archaeologists are people who look for things buried in the earth, which have been leftover from earlier times. They can use these things to build up a picture of life in the past.

Many interesting finds come from graves. Bones can tell us about the age, sex and illnesses of the dead person. Viking graves also contain belongings. The Vikings thought that after death they would go to another world. There they would carry on living the sort of life they had lived on earth. They believed they could take with them the things they would need in the next world, and so these were buried with them.

Archaeologists have also found the remains of Viking houses and ships. Even the most ordinary things, such as Viking rubbish, can tell us something about their way of life.

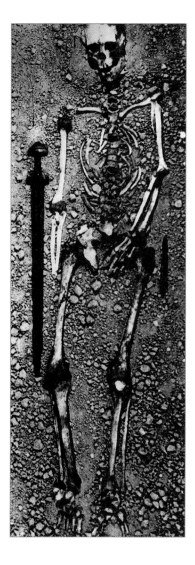

The skeleton of a Viking, buried in the earth with his sword

Viking people

In Viking lands, some people were poor and some were rich. The richest people were known as kings and *jarls*. Then there were warriors, traders, farmers and craftspeople. The poorest people were the slaves, who were called *thralls*.

From the rich to the poor

Names and nicknames

Vikings did not use surnames like we do. Men and women took their fathers' first name as a surname. For example, Leif the son of Erik was known as Leif Eriksson.

Vikings also loved to give each other nicknames. The sagas are full of people with names like Eystein the Noisy, Ulf the Unwashed, Einar Belly-Shaker and Unn the Deep-Minded. The longest nickname of all was given to another Viking king – Halfdan the Generous with Money but Stingy with Food.

Kings and jarls

There were many different rulers in the Viking lands. Most of them were called jarls. When a jarl became very powerful, he might become a king.

Kings and jarls were expected to be generous to their warriors – to give them gifts of swords, cloaks and gold rings. A mean king would soon find his men leaving him – they would look for another ruler to serve. One reason why Viking rulers needed to go raiding was to get treasure for their men.

Thralls

Thralls were people who had been captured on Viking raids and then sold in the market place. It was said that a farm with twelve cows needed three thralls to look after it. Thralls had no rights at all. Their owners could even kill them if they wished. If anyone else killed a thrall, he had to pay the owner what the thrall was worth. In Britain, a thrall was worth eight cows.

Rulers had to be brave fighters, and many of them were killed fighting at the head of their warriors. King Magnus Barefoot, killed in battle at the age of thirty, was supposed to have said, 'kings are made for honour, not for long life.'

Viking rulers liked to have poets, as well as warriors, in their following. Their job was to make up poems praising the ruler's bravery and generosity. Viking rulers loved to listen to such poems while they were feasting.

Thralls were sold in the market place – the scales were used to weigh coins

Viking longships

The Vikings were wonderful ship-builders. Their longships were strong enough to sail the stormy Atlantic Ocean. They were also light and slim enough to be sailed up small shallow rivers. They could be rowed at great speed and then quickly pulled up on to a beach. If they had to, the sailors could even lift them out of the water and drag them overland, from river to river. This meant that Viking raiders could appear without warning, in places where they were least expected.

Ship burials

We know a lot about Viking ships, because important Vikings were buried in them. They believed that they would need them for their journey into the next world.

Many Viking ship burials have been found – archaeologists know where to dig because the ships are covered in great earth mounds. Usually the wood has completely rotted away, leaving only rusty nails to show where the ship once was. Luckily, a few of the ships have survived very well.

This is the Gokstad ship, in which a middle-aged Viking ruler was buried with his richest possessions. Look at the **keel**, the big piece of wood along the bottom. The keel makes the ship strong and stops it from tipping sideways. It is curved to make the ship easier to pull out of the water and on to a beach.

The Gokstad ship

Dragons of the sea

The Vikings were very proud of their ships. The ships were decorated to make them look like dragons. At the front (**prow**), was the dragon's head and at the back, the tail. They gave them their own names, such as 'Long Serpent'. They even made up poems about them. A poet called Thjodolf wrote this in praise of a new longship built by King Harald Hard Ruler:

'See where the great longship
Proudly rests at anchor.
Above the prow, the dragon
Lifts its glowing head...
As one, King Harald's warriors
Lift long oars from the water.
On the shore, the women watch,
Wondering at their sea skill.
We shall row, my lady, without tiring
Until our oars are broken,
Or their broad blades lie idle
When the horns blow for battle.'

Life at sea

Life on board a Viking ship was often cold, wet and very uncomfortable. There was little shelter from the rain or from the waves that lashed against the side. The men spent much of the time bailing out water with scoops and buckets.

There was no way of making hot meals, so the Vikings had to make do with cold dried fish, and beer or water from a tub.

At night, the Vikings either camped ashore or they dropped anchor and spread the sail over the ship like a tent. Inside, they slept in the small spaces between the rowing benches. Here they crawled into big sleeping bags made from animal skins. Each bag held two men who were known as 'sleeping bag mates'.

Life could be miserable on board a Viking ship

Running along the oars

A game they played was 'running along the oars'. The oars were put out and a Viking had to try to run along the outside of the ship, jumping from oar to oar without tumbling into the sea. Everyone would laugh when he fell in.

Finding the way

The Vikings had no maps or special equipment for finding the way at sea. Yet they were able to cross seas and oceans, often out of sight of land, and then get home again (look at the map on pages 4 and 5). How did they do it?

Floki Raven

A famous Viking explorer called Floki Raven got his nickname because he took ravens along on one of his voyages. When he was out of sight of land, he released one. It flew high into the sky, where it could see much further than the Vikings down below. The raven circled and came back to the ship, so Floki knew there was no land in sight. Later, another raven flew straight off into the distance because it had seen land. Floki followed it, and discovered Iceland.

Even on the open sea, there are many signs which could help an experienced sailor find his way. He could tell how far to the north or south he was by the position of the Pole Star. The further north you travel, the higher this star appears in the sky.

Sea-birds and sea animals could also help Vikings find out where they were. Whales, for example, gathered to feed a day's sailing south of Iceland. When Vikings sailing to Iceland saw the whales, they knew they were nearly there. Even the changing colour of the water and floating objects, such as twigs, could be signs that land was near.

Despite all their skills, many Vikings drowned at sea and many of their ships were wrecked in storms.

Viking warriors

Every male Viking had to know how to fight. Even at home on his farm, he might need to defend himself against other Vikings. There was a saying that a man should never move an inch from his weapons when working in the fields. He never knew when he would need them.

The most important weapons were swords and battleaxes. Warriors also carried round wooden shields and wore simple helmets. Helmets were usually round, leather caps strengthened with bands of iron. Only the richest warriors could afford an iron helmet or a **shirt of mail.**

Although few Viking helmets have been found, we can tell what they looked like from carvings

Swords

Making a sword took a lot of time and skill. A swordsmith heated bars of iron and then twisted them together before beating them flat. This gave the sword strength so that it would not snap in the middle of a fight. Better quality iron was then used to make the cutting edges.

Swords were highly prized and given names, such as 'life-taker' and 'leg-biter'. Their blades and handles were often richly decorated.

Many swords have been found in Viking graves like the one shown here. (See page 7 also.)

Berserks

The most feared Viking warriors were called **berserks**. They worked themselves up into a crazy state when they went into battle. When they were in this state, no-one could defeat them. We still use the word 'berserk' to mean wild or crazy.

One of the sagas describes a berserk called Ljot:

He was a very big man, strong-looking, and carried a shield and a sword. As he approached the fighting area, his berserk fit came on and he began howling horribly and biting his shield.

A 'berserk' warrior

Berserks always seem to be biting their shields in the sagas, like this chess piece found on the Isle of Lewis. A berserk must have been a terrifying sight!

Leaving a good name

Viking men believed that there was nothing more important than being remembered as a brave warrior. There was a saying that 'Cattle die, kinsmen die, a man himself will die. There is only one thing that does not die, the fame a man leaves behind him.'

One way of being remembered was through poetry. The Vikings made up poems in which they boasted of their skill in war. In this poem, a Viking called Egil Skallagrimson described his raiding deeds:

'I've carried the bloodstained sword
And the slippery spear,
The raven at my right hand
As we raiders went forward.
Burning for battle,
We made their barns blaze.'

The lightning raids

In the year 793, Viking ships appeared on the north-east coast of England. They attacked the monastery of Lindisfarne, robbing it of its treasures. This was the first of many lightning raids on British monasteries.

A carving of Viking raiders from Lindisfarne

A monastery was a place where monks lived. They spent their time in prayer and in making beautiful copies of books, especially the Bible. Monasteries were holy places. The one at Lindisfarne was especially holy because it held the tomb of a famous saint called Cuthbert. Saints were people who had lived such good lives that they were thought to have special powers, even after death.

The Christians of England were horrified that such a holy place could be attacked. Bishop Alcuin of York wrote:

Never before has such a terror appeared in Britain, nor was it thought possible that such an attack from the sea could be made. See the Church of St Cuthbert spattered with the blood of the priests of God and robbed of all its ornaments!

This piece of jewellery, from a woman's grave in Norway, originally came from a book in an English monastery

Why did the Vikings go raiding?

The Vikings were not Christians, so they did not think of monasteries as holy places. They thought that a monastery was a place stuffed with treasure. The monks did not put up a fight so it was easy to take them away as slaves.

To a Viking, a Bible was not a holy book but a thing with beautifully engraved gold on it. This was often ripped off and made into jewellery.

Life as a raider

Soon, Vikings began to settle in islands off Scotland, such as the Orkneys. They used these islands as bases for more raids around Britain. The *Orkney Saga* tells us about the life of a Viking raider called Svein:

Svein would work hard in the spring and have great amounts of seed sown. When this work was done, he would go off and raid the Scottish Isles and Ireland, and he would come home at mid-summer. He called this his 'spring trip'. He would stay at home till the corn had been harvested. Then he would go raiding again, and not come back till the winter. He called this his 'autumn trip'.

X   MONASTERIES AND ABBEYS

↗   VIKING ATTACKS

(Arrows without dates show other attacks made but the dates of these are unknown.)

SHETLAND ISLANDS

ORKNEY ISLANDS

SUTHERLAND CAITHNESS

OUTER HEBRIDES

795 802 805
X

795

793 LINDISFARNE
X
794 JARROW
X
WEARMOUTH 794
X

NORTHUMBRIA
•YORK

795 RATHIN ISLANDS
X

DUBLIN

WEXFORD

MERCIA   EAST ANGLIA

842 851

WESSEX

840
841

838

789 840

n
W   e
s

Early Viking raids on the British Isles

The Great Army

After years of lightning raids, the Vikings began to attack in different ways. Instead of coming in two or three ships, the Vikings started arriving in big fleets. Instead of making quick raids and then sailing home, they began to build camps, and stay over the winter.

In 865, a 'Great Army' of Vikings crossed the sea from Denmark and landed in England. This time, the Vikings had come to stay for good.

The four kingdoms

In those days, England was not a single country. It was a land made up of four separate kingdoms: **Northumbria, East Anglia, Mercia** and **Wessex**. These kingdoms had often been at war with each other. The English kings were not likely to join together to fight the Vikings.

The Great Army arrives in England

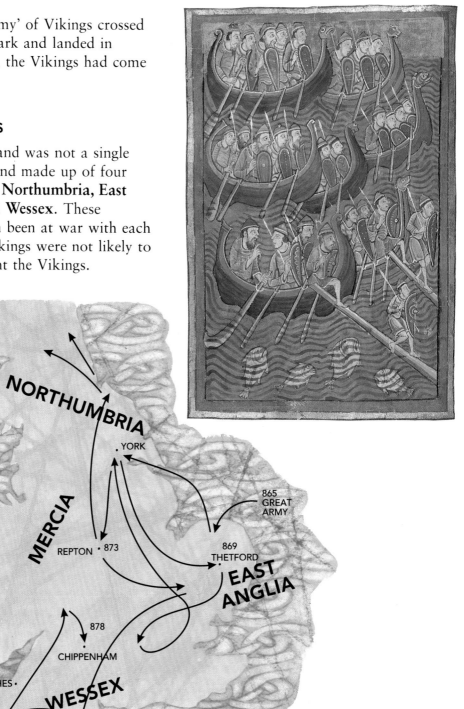

NORTHUMBRIA

YORK

865 GREAT ARMY

REPTON • 873

869 THETFORD

EAST ANGLIA

MERCIA

878

CHIPPENHAM

SOMERSET MARSHES •

WESSEX

Movements of the Great Army

Northumbria

The Great Army attacked each of these kingdoms in turn. First they conquered Northumbria and killed the Northumbrian king, Aella. Then they turned south, towards the other kingdoms.

East Anglia

We know where the Great Army went thanks to a book called the *Anglo-Saxon Chronicle*. This is a year by year history of England, written by Anglo-Saxon monks. Here is their entry for the year 869:

> *In this year, the army rode into East Anglia and made a winter camp at Thetford. The same winter, King Edmund fought against them, and the Danes won the victory. They killed the king and overran the whole kingdom.*

King Edmund is dragged off his throne to be killed

Mercia

In the year 873, Mercia was invaded. Burhred, the king of Mercia, ran away to Italy. He did not want to die like the other two kings.

In Mercia, the Great Army camped for the winter at a place called Repton. Archaeologists have found traces of the Viking camp. The most important find was a grave, which held 249 skeletons. Most were men aged between fifteen and forty-five. Many had war wounds, but these wounds had all healed. This shows they had not died in battle. Perhaps they had died of a disease which had swept the camp.

Wessex

In 878, the Vikings turned on the remaining English kingdom, Wessex. In the middle of winter, when an attack was least expected, they swept on the court of King Alfred of Wessex at Chippenham. Alfred was lucky to escape with a small band of followers.

It looked as if the Vikings had finally conquered all of England.

Alfred of Wessex

In the year 878, the Vikings seemed to be in control of all of England. Of the four English kings, two had been killed and one had run away. The fourth, King Alfred of Wessex, was hiding in the marshes of Somerset. Yet King Alfred refused to give up.

The Battle of Edington

From his hideout in the marshes, Alfred secretly sent messages to the men of Wessex to join him in a new army. In May 878, the army gathered and marched towards the Viking camp.

The Vikings came out to meet them and a great battle was fought at a place called Edington. A monk called Asser described what happened:

Fighting fiercely against the whole Viking army, Alfred won the victory. After beating the Vikings, he chased them back to their fortress. Then he boldly made camp in front of their fortress with all his army. Two weeks later, the Vikings, terrified by hunger, cold and fear, asked for peace.

The peace agreement

The Vikings promised to leave Wessex and their king, Guthrum, agreed to become a Christian. England was now split into two areas. The south and west was the English kingdom of Wessex. The north and east remained in Viking hands. This later became known as the **Danelaw**, the place where Danish rather than English laws were in force.

WESSEX

THE DANELAW

This coin hoard, buried by a Viking, includes more than 7000 coins

Buried treasure

When King Alfred was alive, there were no banks where people could put their money for safety. In times of danger, people buried their money, hoping to dig it up later.

'Coin hoards' are collections of coins and valuables which have been found over the years, often by farmers ploughing their fields. The coins carry the names of kings and thanks to this, they can be dated. The latest date they show is likely to be when they were buried.

People in King Alfred's time often had to hide their money from rival armies. Many coin hoards have been dug up, dating from the time that Viking and English armies were roaming England. Some were buried by English people, fearing the approach of the Vikings. Others were buried by Vikings when it looked like the English were winning. We can tell which is which because Viking hoards have both foreign and English coins, but English hoards only have English coins.

Viking settlers

Once the fighting stopped, the Vikings in the Great Army settled down to farm the land. They stayed in touch with their families and friends back in Denmark. Many of these families came across the sea to join them.

Later, another group of Viking settlers arrived, from Ireland and the north of Scotland. They made their homes in north-west England. Unlike the earlier Danish settlers, these Vikings originally came from Norway. (Look at the map on pages 4 and 5.)

There were now thousands of Viking families living in the British Isles. You can still see signs of these Viking settlers. All you have to do is look at a map.

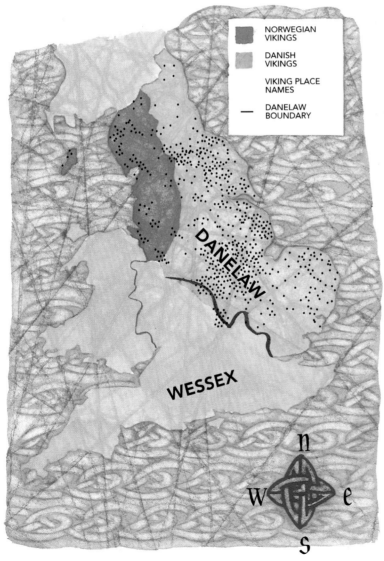

The Vikings settle in England

Map legend:
- NORWEGIAN VIKINGS
- DANISH VIKINGS
- VIKING PLACE NAMES
- DANELAW BOUNDARY

Viking place-names

Before the Vikings arrived, English villages had names ending in 'ham', 'field', 'ing' and 'ton'. The new settlers spoke a different language, and so they had different ways of naming places. Here are the most common Viking place name endings:

by   – a village

thorpe – a tiny village

toft   – a farm

thwaite – a clearing

beck   – a stream

holm   – a small island

tarn   – a small lake

When we see a town or village name with one of these endings, it is a good sign that Vikings once lived there. Many of them even record the name of the man who first settled there. For example, Grimsby was the village of a Viking called Grim.

The dots on this map show the different villages and towns with Viking names. This tells us which parts of England were settled by Vikings.

Viking words in English

In many places, Vikings and English people lived side by side. In time, the English picked up lots of Viking words. We still use around 600 of these words. Among them are 'happy', 'ugly', 'fellow', 'call', 'egg', 'take', 'husband', 'knife' and 'law'.

Clues in stone

The Vikings had their own special style of carving stone, different from the English way. When we find a stone carved in this style, we have another sign of Viking settlers.

In the north of England, almost a hundred Viking stones called **hogbacks** have been found. These are stones carved in the shape of a long house with a curving roof like a Viking farm house. There is usually an animal at each end, often a bear wearing a muzzle. No one is sure what these stones were for, but they were probably grave stones.

Hogback gravestones found in Brompton, North Yorkshire

Farming

The Vikings who came to settle in the British Isles mainly lived on farms, scattered throughout the countryside. Some of their farm buildings have been found by archaeologists. These buildings help us understand what life was like in Viking times.

Jarlshof – a Viking farm

The Shetland Islands, north of Scotland, were one of the first places settled by the Vikings. At Jarlshof, in the Shetlands, archaeologists found the stone walls of a Viking farm under the sand. Vikings had lived there for 400 years, but eventually they had left.

This is what the farm buildings at Jarlshof might have looked like when the Vikings lived there

Farm buildings

The main building was the long house, where the farmer lived with his family. Its walls were made of stone, lined with earth and grass to keep the warmth in. Inside, there was a long hall with a fireplace running down the middle. On each of the curved walls, there was a long, earth bench, covered with stone slabs. The house also had a separate kitchen with an oven built into its wall.

Next to the house was a **byre**, a shed where the cattle were kept at night. There was a barn for hay and a stable for ponies. There was even a small bath house, where the family could take a steam bath, like a sauna.

Archaeologists found the remains of this Viking farm at Jarlshof – the other buildings at the top right were built many years later

Farming, hunting and fishing

Bones found in the rubbish tell us which animals were kept on the farm: cattle, sheep, pigs and ponies. Other bones show that the people did not just live by farming. Whale, seal and cod bones tell us that they fished at sea and red deer bones show that they hunted on the land as well.

Making things

The people of Jarlshof had to make almost everything they needed. They made their own clothes with the wool from their sheep. They also had to make and repair all the tools they used on the farm. One of the buildings was a **smithy**, a workshop for making things out of iron.

Archaeologists made a wonderful find right in the middle of the city of York. From 1976 to 1981, they dug beneath an area called Coppergate and found the remains of a Viking city.

The Vikings called the city of York **Jorvik**. Between 866 and 954, it was the capital of a Viking kingdom. The city was already very old when the Vikings arrived, but it doubled in size under their rule.

The remains of a Viking city found in Coppergate, York

The buildings in Jorvik in Viking times

City buildings

The buildings of the city of Jorvik were close together, separated by narrow walkways. Two types of building were found. The oldest were made of **wattle**, twigs tightly woven around upright posts. Later, Viking buildings were made with oak planks which made them stronger. Fire is a big risk with closely-packed wooden buildings. Layers of ash showed that the buildings had burned down and been rebuilt several times.

The backyards

The archaeologists found deep pits in the backyards. Some of them, lined with wood, were used as wells. Others, with wattle lining, were for storage. There were also cesspits which were used as toilets. In these backyards, Viking families kept small, dark, hairy pigs in wattle pens.

Archaeologists clean a Viking pit

Jorvik would have seemed a very dirty place to us. There were no rubbish collectors and rotting rubbish piled up faster than people could bury it. The wells were dug so close to the cesspits that the water wasn't fit to drink. All the people of Jorvik suffered from **gut-worms**, animals which lived in their stomachs. The eggs of the worms were found in the cesspits.

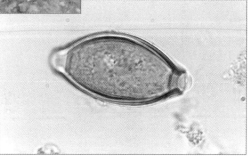

This egg came from a worm that once lived in a Viking's stomach!

Trade and crafts

We usually think of Vikings as fierce warriors and raiders. We often forget that much of their time was spent as peaceful traders and craftspeople. The Vikings were always interested in trade. They had contacts all over Europe, as well as the best merchant ships around.

Ireland

It was in Ireland that Viking trade had the biggest effect. Before the Vikings arrived, the Irish lived in villages rather than towns and they did not trade with other countries. Thanks to the Vikings, trading towns sprang up all around the Irish coast. **Dublin, Limerick, Waterford** and **Wicklow** were all Viking settlements. These were the very first proper towns in Ireland.

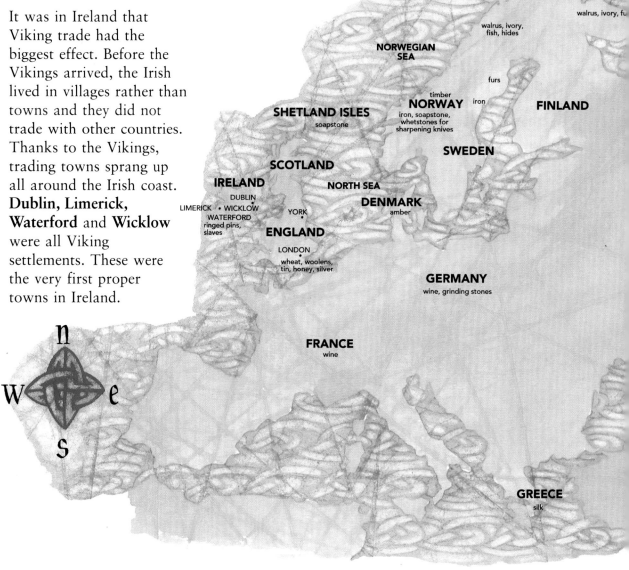

walrus, ivory, fu

walrus, ivory, fish, hides

NORWEGIAN SEA

furs

timber

NORWAY

iron

FINLAND

iron, soapstone, whetstones for sharpening knives

SHETLAND ISLES

soapstone

SWEDEN

SCOTLAND

IRELAND

NORTH SEA

DUBLIN

DENMARK

LIMERICK • WICKLOW

YORK

amber

WATERFORD

ringed pins, slaves

ENGLAND

LONDON

wheat, woolens, tin, honey, silver

GERMANY

wine, grinding stones

FRANCE

wine

GREECE

silk

Vikings brought things to Jorvik from many different countries

The merchants of Jorvik

The biggest Viking trading centre in England was York, or Jorvik. Around the year 1000, an English monk wrote a description of Jorvik:

A city made rich by the wealth of merchants, who come from everywhere, but especially from the Danish people.

Amber necklace

We can tell that Jorvik was a rich place from the things which the archaeologists have dug up. Vikings brought things to Jorvik from many different countries. **Soapstone**, a soft stone used to make bowls, was brought over the sea from Norway. Germany provided wine and stones for grinding grain into flour (local stones left too much grit). **Amber**, a yellow stone for jewellery, had probably come from Denmark. A cap made from silk had come all the way from Greece.

Workshops

Although there were lots of things from other countries, most things sold in Jorvik were made by local craftspeople. The archaeologists found their workshops with things they had made and thrown away.

There were woodworkers, who made bowls and cups, and leatherworkers who made shoes. There was a workshop for making combs out of antlers and bones. There were also jewellers making metal brooches and amber necklaces.

Some of the objects help us understand the way the craftspeople worked. This cow rib (below) was used by a jeweller to practise making a pattern before cutting it on metal.

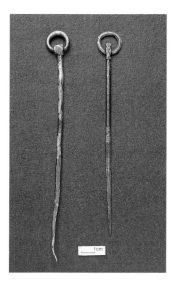

These ringed pins were brought to Jorvik from Ireland

At home

This is what the inside of one of the Jorvik houses might have looked like. It had one big room, used for cooking, eating, working and sleeping. In the middle was a fireplace with a stone floor where a fire was kept burning. This gave warmth and light to the house, and it was used for cooking. The open fire must have made the room very smoky.

The floor was made of earth, stamped hard and spread with straw. The walls were wood or wattle. They were covered with rugs or animal skins to keep out the wind.

There were no cupboards and so the room was cluttered with objects. Tools and weapons hung from the walls and ceilings. Food was stored in tubs on the floor. Valuables and clothes were kept in locked wooden chests.

Around the walls ran a long, earth bench with sides made of wood or wattle. At night, this bench was spread with rugs and it was used as a bed for all the family. Only the richest people had separate bedrooms. It was more important to keep warm than to have your own room.

The inside of a Viking room

What did people eat?

Thanks to the archaeologists, we have a good idea of the sort of food that Vikings liked. Shells and bones from the rubbish in Jorvik show us the fish and animals that people ate. Seeds found in the pits used as toilets can tell us about fruit and vegetables.

Cattle, sheep, goats, pigs and chickens were all sources of meat. The Jorvik people also liked many types of fish, especially eels, caught locally, and oysters, brought up the river from the sea.

The meat was either boiled in a pot or roasted over the fire on a metal stick. It was often salted, pickled or smoked to stop it going rotten because there were no fridges in Viking times.

The favourite vegetables were onions, cabbages, carrots and peas. People also liked fruit, such as apples and plums. Barley or wheat was made into bread and baked in the ashes of the fire.

Vikings drank milk, home-brewed beer and **mead**, a strong drink made from honey. Richer people drank wine, brought over the sea from Germany.

There were far fewer flavourings then. There was no sugar, but honey was used instead as a sweetener. Some herbs were also used such as dill, coriander and mustard.

Can you see where the fireplace might have been in this picture?

Viking women

Viking women lived very differently to Viking men. They were not expected to fight or to sail longships. But their work was just as hard and took just as much skill.

In the Viking homelands, women had to run the farm while their husbands were away raiding or trading. Many husbands did not return from such trips. They drowned at sea or were killed in battle. Viking women had to be tough and independent.

A mother and her young daughter spinning wool with spindle whorls

Women's work

As well as looking after the house and the children, women had to do all kinds of work around the farm. They milked the cows and made butter and cheese. They harvested the grain from the fields, ground it into flour and baked it into bread.

It was women who made most of the family's clothes. They sheared the sheep and combed the wool to get rid of tangles. Then they spun it into thread, using a weighted piece of wood called a **spindle whorl**. Women also made brightly coloured dyes from various plants. Another plant, **flax**, was used to make linen. They dyed the thread and then wove it into cloth on a **loom**.

From an early age, girls watched and helped their mothers, learning the skills they would need when they grew up.

Belongings

We can tell a lot about women's lives from things found in their graves. Just as Viking men were buried with their weapons, women were buried with their most important belongings – the things they would need in the next world.

These objects (below) were found in the grave of a young woman and her new-born baby in Orkney. She had died soon after giving birth, which happened a lot in Viking times.

You can see the shears she used to clip wool from the sheep as well as her wool comb for untangling knots. At the top left is her sickle for harvesting grain. You can also see her comb and her jewellery, including a valuable brooch with a long pin. Bronze strap ends were used as decoration on belts.

Leaving a good name

Many carved stones have been found which were set up in memory of wives and daughters. The messages written on them tell us the qualities that Vikings admired in women.

One stone, set up by a woman called Gunvor in memory of her daughter Astrid, says, 'She was the most nimble-fingered girl in Hadeland'. Another stone, set up by a man in memory of his wife, says, 'No better mistress will come to Hassmyra to look after the farm'.

part of a knife   sickle   weaving sword   wool comb

oval brooches

shears

comb

part of a wool comb

bone tool

whale bone

necklace   brooch with long pin   strap ends

Games and stories

The Vikings had many different ways of having a good time. They loved all kinds of sports, especially those which could show off their strength. Grown ups and children ran races, wrestled, swam and played games with bats and balls. They also gambled with dice and played at board games. Boards and pieces have been found by archaeologists in several Viking digs.

These bone pieces from a Viking game were found in Jorvik

Feasts

Feasts were the most popular Viking entertainment. They were held for any excuse. For the host, it was a way of showing how rich and generous he was. A good feast could last for days.

The aim of a feast was to eat and drink as much as possible. People drank beer and mead from cattle horns, which were passed from one drinker to another. At the same time, there were often entertainers such as jugglers, acrobats and musicians, who played on small harps. Ordinary people made their own music too, using whistles made from bird bones.

A Viking feast

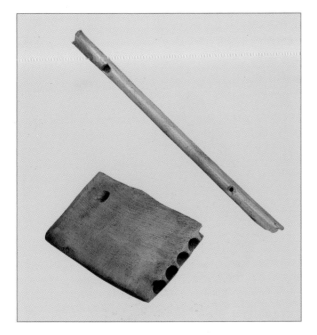

A whistle made from a bird's leg and pan pipes from the Jorvik dig

Poetry

During the feasts, men and women took turns at reciting poems, as well as making them up on the spot. The Vikings loved poetry which described things in new and unusual ways. For example, instead of saying, 'the ship sailed the sea', a Viking poem would say something like, 'the horse of the waves rode the whale road'. This means that a lot of Viking poems are very hard to understand!

Children's games

Children made their own games and toys. They floated pieces of wood in ponds, pretending they were longships, and they made small farm buildings out of mud. They played at the sort of things they would have to do as grown ups.

Halfdan and Harald

In one of the sagas, two brothers, Halfdan and Harald, were playing beside a pond. Halfdan was playing at being a farmer while Harald was floating toy warships made of wood. King Olaf of Norway stopped to chat with them, asking the boys what they would most like when they grew up.

'Cattle', replied Halfdan.

'How many cattle would you like?' asked King Olaf.

'So many', said Halfdan, 'that when they went to drink, they would stand shoulder to shoulder around the whole lake.'

'What would you like to own most of?' King Olaf asked Harald.

'Warriors', answered Harald.

'How many warriors?' asked the king.

'So many', replied Harald, 'that they would eat all Halfdan's cattle up in one meal!'

Gods and religion

The Vikings believed in many different gods. These gods were in charge of different things. Frey, for example, was a god of farming. He provided the sunshine and rain which made the crops grow. His sister Freya was the goddess of love and marriage.

Thor

The most popular god of all was **Thor**, the red-bearded god of thunder. Thor was not clever, but he was very strong and brave. Thor spent most of his time fighting giants. His magic weapon was a stone hammer, called **Mjolnir** ('the destroyer') which he grasped with a pair of iron gloves. Thor also had a magic belt which doubled his strength as soon as he put it on.

Thor travelled in a cart pulled by two he-goats. Whenever he was hungry, he would kill, cook and eat one of the goats. The next morning, he only had to touch the goatskin with his hammer and the goat would come back to life.

Many Vikings believed that Thor could bring them good luck. They wore tiny hammers around their necks, and gave their children names which included 'Thor' such as Thora or Thorolf.

Thor, god of thunder

Odin

The most powerful and mysterious god was **Odin.** He was the god of war, wisdom, magic and poetry. Odin only had one eye – he had given the other away to pay for drinking the magic water of wisdom. Odin had many strange powers. He could turn himself into a bird, a snake or a fish. He also had an eight-legged horse called **Sleipnir** which could outrun any other animal.

Odin lived in a great hall called **Valhalla,** where he welcomed brave warriors who had died in battle. In Valhalla, they were always feasting and playing warlike games.

Odin's horse Sleipnir, riding to Valhalla, carved on a Viking's tombstone

Sacrifices

The Vikings believed that they could win the help of the gods by giving them sacrifices. A sacrifice was a gift. It could be a person, an animal or a treasured possession. A slave or an animal such as a goat was killed as a gift to the gods.

Warriors gave sacrifices to Odin to ask him for victory, and then to thank him if he provided it. Sacrifices were also given to Frey, to ask him for a good harvest or a mild winter. When a warrior died, slaves were sometimes sacrificed and buried with him. This was so they could carry on serving him in the next world.

A Viking sacrifice – the bones of 20 animals were found with some Viking metalwork at Skerne, in Humberside

Christianity

In Britain, France and Germany, the Vikings found people who followed a very different kind of religion – Christianity. The Christians were horrified by the Vikings' religion and they made every effort to make them give it up.

Missionaries and kings

The Christian Church sent many missionaries to the Vikings. Missionaries were holy men who tried to convince the Vikings that their old religion was wrong. This is the sort of argument they used:

Stop worshipping false gods and serving the devil, for your gods are made with human hands and are deaf, dumb and blind. How can they save you when they cannot save themselves?

King Harald Bluetooth is baptised

This is part of a message sent to King Horik of Denmark. For the church, it was very important to try to make kings believe in Christianity. Once they had become Christian, Viking kings would try to force their people to follow their religion. They built churches and smashed the carvings of the old gods.

Viking kings saw that becoming Christian could make them more powerful. As Christians they would be treated as equals by the Christian kings of Europe.

When a king became Christian, he was **baptised** – sprinkled with holy water as a sign that he accepted the new religion. Here you can see the baptism of King Harald Bluetooth of Denmark.

The hammer and the cross

It was a long time before the Vikings all gave up their old beliefs. For a while, they believed in two religions at the same time. The smith's mould on the right was used for making both Thor's hammers and Christian crosses.

A smith's mould from Denmark

Many people must have felt like Helgi the Lean, a Viking described in one of the sagas:

Helgi was very mixed in his beliefs. He believed in Christ, yet he asked Thor for help on sea voyages and when facing danger, and for everything which struck him as of real importance.

Eventually people gave up wearing Thor's hammer for luck; they wore the Christian cross instead. Christianity brought many changes to Viking life. Once they had become Christians, Vikings stopped making sacrifices and they were no longer buried with their belongings. They became more like the people who lived in the rest of Europe. As Christians, it was much easier for Vikings in Britain to live at peace with the British.

Runes and art

Although the Vikings did not write books, they did have their own sort of writing, called *runes*. Runes were letters which were mainly made up of straight lines. This made them easy to carve on wood, stone or bone.

Here is the Viking alphabet, called the **Futhark** (or **Futhork**) after its opening letters.

It took time to carve runes, and so they were only used for short messages. One use was to write the owner's name on an object. For example, a sword found in Ireland had 'Dufnall Sealshead owns this sword' scratched on it.

Bone comb-case with the maker's name scratched on

The runes on this comb-case, found in Lincoln, say 'Thorfastr made a good comb'. Can you make out the word 'Thorfastr' on the right-hand side?

Magic spells

The Vikings believed that runes had magic powers. They could be used to cure illnesses or to make a curse – a spell bringing bad luck to an enemy. They could even be used to make someone fall in love with you.

Love runes

Egil's Saga tells the story of Egil Skallagrimson, a Viking skilled at carving magic runes. One day he was asked to treat a woman called Helga who had been sick in bed for days. Her father had got a young man to carve some runes for her, but these had not done any good.

Egil searched under Helga's pillow and found the runes the man had carved. He could see at once that they were the wrong sort of runes. In fact, they were love runes. The man who carved them had asked Helga to marry him, but she had refused. He had then cut the runes to make her fall in love with him, but he did not have the skill. His runes had made her illness even worse.

Egil burned the whalebone on which the runes were carved and then cut a new set of healing runes, which he put under Helga's pillow. She started to get better at once!

Viking art

Viking artists were skilled in working metal, stone, wood and bone. They loved to mix rich patterns with the shapes of strange animals. These patterns are often so complicated that it takes a while to make out the shape of the animal.

Can you see the animals in these carvings?

The raids for Danegeld

Between 901 and 937, the part of England called the Danelaw was slowly reconquered by the English. For the first time, England was a single kingdom under one king. The Viking settlers stayed living in the Danelaw, but they were now ruled by English rather than Viking kings.

For nearly 80 years, England was free from Viking attacks. However, the English had not seen the last of the Viking longships.

Danegeld

In the 980s, the Viking ships came back, making a new series of lightning raids. This time, their aim was to get the English to pay them money not to attack them. This money, which the English paid again and again, was called **Danegeld**.

Swedish Vikings

The Vikings who took part in the raids came from all over the Viking homelands. For the first time, Swedish Vikings took part in the attacks. We know this because of rune stones, found in Sweden.

This stone was set up for a Viking called Ulf when he died. The message carved on the dragon's back says, 'Ulf has taken Danegeld three times in England'. It also shows the names of the Vikings who led the three raids – Toste, Thorkel and Cnut (Knutr).

A rune stone with carved message

The Battle of Maldon

One Viking raid is described in a famous Anglo-Saxon poem called 'The Battle of Maldon'.

In 991, a Viking fleet sailed up the River Blackwater to Maldon in Essex. They landed on an island, separated from Maldon by a narrow, raised **causeway**. Before the Vikings could cross the causeway, an English army had arrived, led by a man called Byrhtnoth. The two armies now watched each other across the narrow stretch of water.

One of the Vikings crossed the causeway with a message:

> *Bold seafarers have sent me to you,*
> *ordered me to tell you that you must quickly send*
> *gold rings in return for protection. And it is better for you*
> *all that you should buy off these spears with money*
> *than that we should join battle so harmfully.*

Here you can see where The Battle of Maldon was once fought

Byrhtnoth refused to pay the Danegeld and got his men ready for battle. The Vikings said that the English should let them come across the causeway, so that they could have a fair fight. Byrhtnoth agreed. The 'wolves of slaughter', as the poem calls the Vikings, rushed across to the mainland.

In the fighting that followed, Byrhtnoth and most of his men were killed. The Vikings then sailed off to try somewhere else for Danegeld.

Cnut – Viking King of England

In the year 1016, there was a new invasion of England by a huge Viking army. It was led by Cnut (also known as Canute), King of Denmark. After fierce fighting, Cnut made peace with the English king, Edmund Ironside. They agreed to share the kingdom between them. When Edmund died soon after, Cnut was made king and for the first time, a Viking ruled the whole of England.

What was Cnut like?

In some ways, Cnut was a typical Viking ruler. He led his warriors into battle, and he had his own hired poets to praise his deeds. This is what one of Cnut's poets said about him:

> *Generous giver of mighty gifts,*
> *You will lose your life before your courage fails.*

In other ways, Cnut was more like an English king. He was a Christian, and he gave lots of money to the Church. This picture shows Cnut and his queen, giving a beautiful gold cross to the Church at Winchester. It also tells us how Cnut wanted people to think of him.

Cnut grips his sword, to show that he is a strong ruler and the angel holding his crown shows that his royal power comes from God

Cnut and the waves

Cnut is best known for a story that he ordered his throne to be placed on the sea-shore, just as the tide was rising. In front of his puzzled followers, he then spoke to the waves:

This land which I sit on is mine. No one has ever disobeyed my orders and got away with it. I therefore order you not to rise over my land, and not to dare to wet the clothes or legs of your lord.

Of course, the sea rose as always and gave Cnut a soaking.

This might show that Cnut was a stupid and proud king but the story did not end with the soaking. Cnut then jumped up and told his followers:

See how empty the power of kings is! Only God is worthy of being called a king, for only He can command the earth and the sea.

Cnut wanted the sea to rise, to teach his followers not to be big-headed.

Whether the story ever took place is another question. It was written down 100 years after Cnut's death, by a monk called Henry of Huntingdon.

Cnut speaks to the waves

1066 – end of the Viking age

We remember 1066 as the year in which England was conquered by the Normans under William the Conqueror. We often forget that 1066 was also the year of another invasion – the last great Viking invasion of England.

The warring brothers

King Edward of England died in 1066, leaving no son to follow him. The most powerful man in England, Earl Harold Godwinsson, now made himself king.

Harold's younger brother, Tostig, felt he should be king instead. So he sailed to Norway to ask help from a famous Viking, King Harald Hard Ruler. The Viking king agreed to help Tostig, for he was also planning to be king in England.

In September 1066, the great Viking fleet arrived in the north of England. King Harold Godwinsson rushed to meet them with his army. He found them at Stamford Bridge, near York.

A Viking saga says the English Harold sent a message to his brother asking for peace and offering to share the kingdom. Tostig replied by asking him what he would give Harald Hard Ruler. Harold Godwinsson answered that he would give the Viking just enough English soil for a grave.

With that, the battle began. It was a disaster for the Viking army. Both Tostig and the Viking king were cut down by the English swords. Of the 300 ships invading, only 24 sailed back to Norway.

The Norman invasion

Harold Godwinsson had no time to celebrate after his victory over Tostig. News came that another great army had arrived in his kingdom, on the south coast.

This was the army of William of Normandy. The Normans were Vikings who had settled in Northern France. They had given up their old language and now spoke French. In other ways though, they were still Vikings. They sailed across the English Channel in dragon-headed ships, as you can see in this picture from the **Bayeux Tapestry**, made to celebrate William's invasion.

The Battle of Hastings

On 14 October 1066, the tired English soldiers fought another great battle at Hastings, and lost.

England was now ruled by the Normans, strong rulers with a powerful army. There were no more great Viking invasions and so 1066 is often seen as the end of the Viking Age. Even so, there were still Viking raids from time to time. The last raid of all took place in 1151.

The Normans are coming!

Published by BBC Educational Publishing,
Woodlands, 80 Wood Lane,
London W12 0TT

First published 1993
Reprinted 1995, 1996
© Peter Chrisp/BBC Enterprises Ltd 1993
The moral right of the author has been asserted.

Paperback ISBN: 0 563 35259 0
Hardback ISBN: 0 563 35260 4

Colour reproduction by Daylight Colour, Singapore
Cover origination in England by Goodfellow and Egan
Printed and bound by BPC Consumer Books Ltd

Photo credits
Aerofilms **p. 25**; Ancient Art and Architecture Collection **pp. 10/11, 14,
16 (below)**; The British Library **p. 44** *Stowe 944 f.6*; The British
Museum **pp. 15, 21, 40**; by permission of the Syndics of Cambridge
University Library **p. 6** *Ff.1.27*; C. M. Dixon **p. 37 (top)**;
Robert Harding Picture Library **p. 36**; English Heritage **p. 16 (top)**;
Michael Holford **pp. 14/15, 46/47**; Humberside County Council
Archaeology Unit **p. 37 (bottom)**; James Lang **p. 23**; Nationalmuseet,
Copenhagen/Niels Elswing **p. 38**; National Museum of Ireland **p. 7
(below)**; The Trustees of the National Museums of Scotland 1993
p. 33; National Trust Photographic Library/Joe Cornish **p. 43**; The
Pierpont Morgan Library, New York **pp. 18** *M.736, f.9v*, **19** *M. 736,
f.12*; Riksantikvaren, Norway/Jac Bruun **p. 41 (top)**;
Riksantikvarieämbetet, Sweden/Bengt A. Lundberg **p. 42**; Stofnun Árna
Magnússonar á Íslandi **p. 7 (top)** *GKS 1005 f.310v*; University Museum
of National Antiquities, Oslo, Norway/T. Teigen **p. 41 (bottom)**; Werner
Forman Archive **p. 39**; York Archaeological Trust Historical Picture
Library **pp. 26, 27, 29, 31, 34, 35**.
Front cover: Nationalmuseet, Copenhagen/Niels Elswing: An animal
head from a wooden harness bow from Søllested, Denmark.

Illustrations © Philip Hood 1993 (pages 8, 9, 11, 12/13, 24, 26,
30/31, 32, 34, 40 and 45) © Brent Linley 1993 (pages 2/3, 4/5, 17,
18, 20, 22 and 28).